BACK
IN THE
ANIMAL KINGDOM

ALSO BY
NEIL HARRISON

Story (chapbook)
In a River of Wind
Into the River Canyon at Dusk

BACK
IN THE
ANIMAL KINGDOM

POEMS BY
NEIL HARRISON

PINYON PUBLISHING

Montrose, Colorado

Cover Painting by Neil Harrison, Photographed by
Julie Ptacek-Wilkey and Jason Elznic

Photograph of Neil Harrison by Mahaila Ramold

First Edition: June 2011

Pinyon Publishing
23847 V66 Trail, Montrose, CO 81403
www.pinyon-publishing.com

Library of Congress Control Number: 2011930992
ISBN: 978-1-936671-02-1

Acknowledgments

Grateful acknowledgment to the editors of the following publications in which some of the poems in this collection first appeared:

In Other Words: "Somewhere This Morning."

Midwest Quarterly: "Old Habits."

Nebraska Life: "Because," "Navy-Blue Pigeon with Half-White Wings," "Waiting for the Cranes."

Owen Wister Review: "Pointing Her West."

Paddlefish: "There is a Fountain Filled with Blood," "The Walking Wounded."

Paterson Literary Review: "On the Block Where I Live," "Once More to the Lake," "The Horses of Hazelwood," "A Spring Day."

Platte Valley Review: "and Golden Needles," "Old Photo of 'Eddie'," "Platte Valley Girls," "This Animal," "This Dog Hunts."

South Dakota Review: "Back in the Animal Kingdom," "The Long Act of Falling," "Wolf-Song Heart," "This Wild Place."

The American Voice: the Legacy of Whitman, Williams, and Ginsberg, a publication of The Poetry Center at Passaic County Community College: "Black-and-White."

The Whoosh Factor: The Astonishing Power of a Generative Writing Group (anthology presently in production): "New Years Eve," "The First Time."

"Water and soil and wind,
color and light and heat:

something forever plump and firm
above the ground,
the urge forever
of something small but ripening

underneath."

—Wm. Kloefkorn, "Nebraska:
This Place, These People"

CONTENTS

I. STRANGE FAMILIAR

II. BACK IN THE ANIMAL KINGDOM

III. THIS WILD PLACE

I. STRANGE FAMILIAR

"What is the knocking at the door in the night?
It is somebody wants to do us harm.

No, no, it is the three strange angels.
Admit them, admit them."

—D. H. Lawrence, "Song of a Man Who Has
Come Through"

STRANGE FAMILIAR

The car door opens and she's off,
perusing another chapter of the world,
nose to the earth, reading whatever
wrote itself down the nearest trail,

this strange, familiar animal,
wire-hair gray as old pages
bound between German-chocolate covers,
her inquisitive head and quivering tail.

She trots through a cottonwood shelterbelt,
a stand of bluestem, patch of cocklebur,
bounds through tangled Canary grass
and dog-tracks across a bar to the water,

wades in, flops down on her belly,
laps her fill and leaps to her feet,
shakes hard, and a sudden mist
arrays her in Loup River silver.

A SPRING DAY

for Leon

I touch the scar this autumn morning
and feel it all flood back again—
that spring day and you, my friend,
dead these many years.

After a week of hard rains
we stood on the trestle south of town,
saw rafts of snags, whole cottonwoods
surfing the crest of the swollen river.

The current cut deep into the north bank
and washed back against the rock rail-bed
as far as Gerhold's gravel pit,
and all along that stretch of ditch

the muddy water boiled with V's,
giant tails and gray-green backs,
some dozen buffaloes up from the river,
spawning in the flooded grass.

We rushed to the car and into town,
found your father's spear, my fishing bow,
then back out, we stalked to the water,
doffed our shoes and went at them,

each taking one of the biggest fish, then
chasing the others as they ripped away
down the murky shallows and out
into the foaming Elkhorn,

something quick and sharp underfoot
as we harried them to the river, and there
saw the gash, the spurting blood,
my red tracks painted on the sand.

We closed the cut with tape off the bow-reel
and laughed at my sudden limp, as I
carried the bow and spear while you
hauled those two great fish to the car,

and still riding that wild rush
we roared back to town in my GTO,
windows down, stereo blaring, speakers
throbbing out *Spirit in the Sky*.

PUTTING ON THE COFFEE,
RE-ENTERING THE NIGHT

"Man's mind, like the expanding universe itself, is engaged in pouring over limitless horizons . . . it betrays all the miraculous unexpectedness which we try vainly to eliminate from the universe."
—Loren Eiseley, "Strangeness in the Proportion," *The Night Country*

From the kitchen window this sky appears
blue as the oceans on an atlas or a globe,
those shallow attempts to map out our place
in a world too deep to comprehend,
where Earth somehow still seems the center
and that warm, cloudless stretch of morning
the true-blue color of the sky, though

on clear nights the boundless dark
burns away illusion, sets us spinning
out once more into the awe-filled everlasting,
where long-gone stars somehow still glow
in that black space beyond this blue
we've grown so long accustomed to
in the dim confines of our cave.

During the day.
the earth seems
singular.
Night fall pulls
away the illusion.

Poem about the snow Globe
young - 3 yrs old
Neer seen snow
Tiny world.
Blue - unreal color

5

THEIR DAYS BEGAN IN THE DARK

Hoarse whispers, tired moans,
creak of bedsprings,
rustle of clothes,
sliver of light under the door,

the quiet clumping of shoes,
scrape of a chair on the kitchen floor,
scratch of a wooden match near the stove,
hiss of gas, *woof* into flame,

clink of a pot, running water,
low whispers punctuated by a cough,
the faint scent of burning gas,
hint of smoke from his *Lucky*,

soon the aroma of coffee
perking loud on the stove,
clunk of cups on the table,
splash of liquid from the pot,

voices humming now,
cough growing louder,
another scrape of chair on floor,
footsteps crossing the porch,

screen door squeaking open and
*clap-clapp*ing shut,
his whistle fading off to the east,
the barn and the morning milking,

clatter of pans in the cupboard,
heavy thunk on the stove,
soon the sizzle
and scent of frying bacon,

the boy, silent, in his bed, staring
through a window at the Sandhills sky,
liquid black as a pool of old oil
splashed with the Milky Way.

NAVY-BLUE PIGEON WITH HALF-WHITE WINGS

Stopped for the light at the intersection,
Fifth Street and Madison Avenue,
I see something kite-like drifting between
the Sacred Heart Church and Courtesy Ford.

All at once out of the church's shadow
in the narrow band of the avenue light
it bursts into sudden living color, a royal-blue
bird fanning white-tipped wings,

an explosive flash over the street one instant
gone as a risen phoenix the next.

SMOKE

No camera quick enough to record it,
no words for colors deep enough to paint
the grasses, yuccas, scattered flowers,
that bottomless blue beyond the lone
sharptail folding at the shot and falling
toward a hill across a ditch where
a blur of fur launches herself and
suddenly it all makes sense—
bird falling, dog mid-leap, your heart
beating wild as the earth beneath
the paws of one of her predators
homing in on one of her prey—
a flash out of nowhere, and gone like *that*,
too quick in every sense for a camera,
and far too full for a thousand words.

what is the story told in
the lightning flick of
a shutter. Five hundredths
of a second full of life;
Eagle, wings in full flap,
Talons on the speckled
of a rainbow trout,
A buck, standing in shadow
on meadow's edge
listening, smelling for death.

AN AUGUST EVENING

On a canvas chair at one end of the porch
he runs his fingers through striped gray fur,
Harley or Davidson purring on his lap,
the tan nanny goat and big white billy
on a ragged couch at the other end
lazing in the shade of the overhang.

His wire-haired pointer lies on her side
a few feet from the screened front door
on this, his place, for a time at least,
four miles out from the nearest town,
small white house, big blue barn,
towering row of ponderosas.

A rust-brown wealth of rotting apples
under the limbs of a stunted tree
draws bees, wasps and butterflies
all afternoon to the sick-sweet scent,
until in the shadows the crickets start,
and doe and fawn cross the road above the creek,

wary of the odd mix of scents,
the dog, the goats, the horses in the pasture,
his beer perhaps, the cigar he smokes
as he stares west over silhouetted grass
high on the hills across the road
at the sun going down on it all.

THIS DOG HUNTS

She lies in the shade west of the garage,
scanning the sky, scenting the morning,
out on the lawn I mowed yesterday
before our run down the hike-and-bike trail,

that section closed now, after the flood,
where I turned her loose as a wish on the world
and she sprinted down the nearly unmarred trail,
every mark erased by last night's rain

but a few fresh tracks of deer and coyote, and
no doubt those pheasants she broke from the trail
and burrowed through the waist-high grass to point,
before my approach sent them clawing skyward.

It's September now, and all she wants
is to be out there, because . . .

FORTY-FOUR SUNSETS

to the memory of Antoine de Saint-Exupéry

Goodbye once more to the darkening sky
as the clouds grow thick and the stars soon lie
hidden so well I can scarcely hear
the music of those bells that once rang clear,
notes so bright against the desert night
the whole sky hovered, a florescent kite
spanning the heavens, light beaming down
those endless miles to this barren ground,
where even near the well now nothing grows
but the faint memory of a distant rose
and the gardener who tamed and cares for it
while I count sunsets, unable to quit
until the stars break through finally
and reveal, once more, his majesty.

LATE MARCH BLIZZARD

The northbound geese turn south again,
staggered waves of snows and blues
deciding to give it another week or two,

as a puffed-up robin scurries stiff-legged
across the walk to the front-yard cedar
and hunkers under its thick white quilt.

But these other guys flutter like black leaves
down to the drifts beneath the maple and
chatter as they bob and weave about,

the only weathercocks today
in perfect tune with the equinox,
these starlings in the snow.

WAITING FOR THE CRANES

There's a boom-town out on the local lake,
augers roaring, shanties popping up,
dozens of fishermen kneeling on the ice,
jigging for panfish with two-foot rods.

It's fifty degrees, second week in March,
and I'm chipping my spud through a foot of ice
to set out another tip-up, hoping
a northern passes by and takes my bait.

Just a week ago long lines of geese
were headed south on a blizzard wind;
now, here and there a hopeful robin
probes for worms in the shoreline grass.

So it goes in Nebraska, every year
the worst and best times battle it out
in these tentative days the weathermen dread
either side of the vernal equinox.

Though in a week or two we'll be looking up
as a heavenful of southbound harbingers
aims their singular prayer at the Platte,
calling the season down.

APRIL EMERGING

She kicks off the cold white sheets at last,
all naked limbs, ready buds, returning

birds puffed full of themselves, as she opens
the gentle petals of the rose, and a scent

from the first sweet garden of the world
makes perfect sense of it all.

ONCE MORE TO THE LAKE

"Summertime, oh summertime, pattern of life
indelible, the fadeproof lake, the woods unshatterable,
the pasture with the sweetfern and the juniper forever
and ever, summer without end."
—E.B. White, "Once More to the Lake"

After Sunday school, that weekly penance,
fat church nodding in a stained-glass dusk,
we'd rush home and wait for a savior to guide us
back into the holy light of day,
and always he'd come
grinning like the devil, red
cheeks smoking, a Chesterfield chimney,
round, bald, buck-toothed Saint Nick
and his wife Ann, the pair so short
they could barely see over
the spacious dash of his big gray Olds
(Delta 88, Body by Fischer), great
trunk stocked like a supermarket shelf
though we'd somehow wedge in fishing gear,
climb aboard those wide suede seats
and hurry west through that ancient gate
the church had tried but failed again to burn
out of the east-most reach of Eden.

TELL 'EM CHARLIE SENTCHA

In those no-school, hot dog days of summer,
my brother and I would pester one another
or our sister long enough to finally
badger Mom into driving us out
to the tracks that led to the trestle,

and we'd lug a load of camping gear
north to the bridge that spanned the river,
where Joel'd lay claim to his favorite spot
by divvying me a share of the smokes
he'd pilfered from *Charlie's Cigars* that morning.

He'd always take the northeast pier,
where the current curled through a deep, black hole,
no doubt picturing some monster catfish
on the bottom, looking up like Charlie Tuna
praying for a bait to descend from above,

and I'd always claim he got the better spot,
happy as a pig in a puddle, with smokes
enough to grin and wear it all night
on my perch on the southwest pier,
where I was pretty sure to catch more fish,

because most were small and would avoid his hole
as carefully as he'd avoided Charlie's gaze
while filching our supply of cheap Coronas
before ducking out again into the alley,
where I was keeping an eye on the back,

and watching Charlie through a barred window,
though he'd never look up, focused as he was
on some fold-out photo in a slick magazine,
while we sailed off like the Starkist crew
whispering, "Sorry Charlie."

SMOKE (NO MIRRORS)

The first day of school after summer break,
it's no real surprise when he comes home to find
the sofa cushions strewn about the living room floor—
his dog Smoke's a wire-haired pointer and
they tend to be wired pretty tight.

But the second day there's a dozen magazines
spread about in a circle on the rug
where it appears some renowned historian
might have just stepped out for a well-earned break
after a long afternoon of intense research.

His high-strung historian out in the yard,
he kneels to re-rack *Nebraska Life*
and finish his chocolate Moo-Latte.
Then he lets her well-read behind back in
so she can lick out the cup while he tries a nap.

But the nap's interrupted by a loud thumping
as she tosses her various toys about, and
he's thinking she's probably right—it's been
over a year since his knee went out—about time
they got back to jogging after school.

In his running shoes and dressed for action,
he does a few stretches before the short drive west,
out to the bike trail along the river, where
they come upon a speed-texting sleep-walker
who passes by without noticing them.

Then, in the distance, a woman jogging
behind a medium-sized black-and-white dog
with a strange trot, and when they near
he says, "Looks like your dog's limping a little."
She smiles. "He's only got three legs."

And close enough now, he can see it;
her sleek dog has just one hind leg.
"Hit by a car," she says as she passes.
"He sure runs good that way," he calls.
She nods and adds, "Still outruns me."

A little farther on he unsnaps the leash and
they're off, across the trestle over the river
and down the long bike trail between
fencerows ripe with plums, grapes, sunflowers, coneflowers
and beyond, vast fields of golden corn and beans.

Across little bridges over nameless creeks,
west three miles to the feedlot corner, then
around and all the way back to the river,
where Smoke heads down for a drink
while he watches from the trestle.

She swims out into the channel, then
swings around and tries to swim upstream.
He shakes his head, signals her to turn
and go with the current, but she keeps on
paddling against it, getting nowhere.

He comes off the trestle and calls her
to follow as he heads downstream,
but she snags an exposed piece of rip-rap,
pulls herself onto that precarious perch,
and without so much as a look downriver,

lunges hard-headed straight at the bank,
gains a foothold and slowly emerges,
bedraggled Aphrodite shaking off the foam.
She wags her tail; he wags his head
and follows her back to the car.

MY FIRST FICTION TEACHER

Bald on top, substantial at the middle,
wide grin full of great buck-teeth
gone bronze behind an endless chain of Chesterfields,

Nick was a poor kid's dream come true,
summer Santa Claus with a single elf,
his wife Ann, as thin as he was round,

no reindeer, just several hundred horses
powering a big beige Oldsmobile,
his four-door Delta 88, our ride

out to another afternoon at Wendt's,
that defunct gravel pit, our favorite lake,
where clear water funneled down into the deep

and recalled for Nick how years before,
fishing from a boat on Crater Lake, he let out
every inch of his line and *never touched the bottom!*

inspiring an excited proposition from my brother,
as yet unaware of Nick's stark fear of drowning,
"Let's go get a *boat*! and try that *here*!"

With bulging eyes above that big bronze grin,
suddenly wild as my brother with excitement,
Nick came back with his trademark phrase,
"Let's *not*! and *say* we did!"

YOUR EVENTUAL DEATH

As you enter the world beneath the words, each
pregnant breath you stuttered through the years,
may you find at bottom the Creator still
coining deeper chapters in your understanding.

And as you reflect upon the myriad Christs
mirrored in that city of gold clear as glass,
may you recognize at last the only one who is
and always was near enough to save you.

Beneath the broken lines
lay a poetic world
where tree roots dangled
in the air and drank humidity.
grey Stone melted and turned white
Froze into long teeth that hung
From the rusturd roof
and jutted From the black Floor

GO GENTLY ON

for Padma Sambava, Dr. Bob Johnson

Go gently on, beyond the last good night.
Now youth's dim fires no longer hide the day.
Behold within, the dawning of true light.

You've ridden long and far, far out of sight,
and that wild heart you bridled will not stay.
Go gently on, beyond the last good night.

Loosen the reins and let that mount take flight.
Though far from home, it's always known the way.
Behold within, the dawning of true light.

In time the wise find nothing left to fight.
Their words fall softly, striking deep as they
go gently on, beyond the last good night.

Let others judge your ride here wrong or right,
such insignificance fast falls away.
Behold within, the dawning of true light.

And now, that inner beacon burning bright,
leave us the laughter of your love I pray.
Go gently on, beyond the last good night.
Behold within, the dawning of true light!

POINTING HER WEST

We're barely out of town heading west
but already she knows we're after grouse,
whining and wagging in the passenger seat,
then stomping that handy throttle, my knee,
and staring ahead as though she knows
the full weight of a wirehaired pointer
will get us there faster than any otherwise.

I push her butt back down on the seat, but
her front paws rebound onto the dash
and I shrug, speed on, and rest assured
that this, my wild and wooly compadre,
will whine and wiggle the whole way west,
as full of righteous song and dance
as any decent dashboard Jesus.

EISELEY

"the child and its accouterments should have been left
where the parents intended . . . to the endless circling
of the stars"
—Loren Eiseley

The search took you finally
over the impossible reaches,
yesterday and tomorrow, both
thresholds into the dark.

Alone, as always, and lost at last
in the heart of the inner desert,
the most desolate place on earth,
you found what links us all.

At the vertex of joy and sorrow,
in the deepest ruin on the planet,
you stared, awed, at the source
exposed, then covered it again,
and labeled it *enigma*.

THE RELATIVE DIMENSIONS
OF MEMORY

remembering Larry Holland

Two days after Reese said, "Put this up,"
eleven years after your sudden death,
I'm staring at a color photograph
I shot nearly twenty years ago.
In a red-checked shirt, hat, and faded jeans,
you smile past your pipe and a small, wood fire,
a thin stand of lodge-pole pines at your back,
the entire Bridger Wilderness beyond.

And I'm viewing it all once more through the lens,
focusing that camera I packed each time
we hiked into the Wind River Range,
the dimensions dissolving until I'm both
with you there in the high country and
alone down here in the living room.

NEW YEAR'S EVE

I need to scent again
the mountain air

in that high camp
up on Cutthroat Lake,

rise once more
under a nearer sun

and pay homage,
honest as those brilliant fish

kissing each day
that warm window,

the glass-flat surface
where they greet a golden god,

feeding each morning
on the high, pure light.

I need that light,
that god, the sun.

11. BACK IN THE ANIMAL KINGDOM

"It is as though there were a covenant between the animal and the human communities honoring the mystery of nature, which is: <u>life lives by killing.</u> No other way. And it is the one life, in two manifestations, that is living this way, by killing and eating itself."

—Joseph Campbell, "In the Beginning: Origins of Man and Myth," Chapter One, *Transformations of Myth Through Time*

BACK IN THE ANIMAL KINGDOM

in memory of Warren Fine

Half a block east of the highway
bisecting a Nebraska college town
midway along its reach from Manitoba
south down the continent to Mexico,
he reviews the essays he's assigned
concerning issues in the humanities,

as the background din of traffic fades
like the buzz of late-summer cicadas,
and only the occasional odd sound registers—
a siren rousting the neighborhood dogs,
a metallic crunch at the intersection
cutting short a loud screech of tires,

a chorus of bellows or squeals that accompanies
the clatter of hooves on aluminum
as another big rig gears down at the light
and the packed-tight stock inside packs tighter,
sliding together on the shit-slick floors
of a trailer headed for the *packing* plant.

And his sense of the words on the page is lost
as he recalls those days he worked the sales
and the midnight chutes at what once was billed
the *World's Largest Livestock Auction,*
his schooling in the work-force ways of the world
long before he took an academic turn.

He pictures again the cane he used,
the hardwood reinforced with plastic pipe
to ward off splitting and give the proper heft,
and he recalls the weapon-like feel of it,
how he drove those milling herds and stopped
the odd ones that tried to break away,

and the years of his subsequent education
pale like a cut and dried rose
as once again he's brought to face
the requisite cruelty that feeds us all,
our dark root buried out of sight and mind
under tons of slick plastic techno-shit,

and he finds the bright promises of civilization
doomed as that plaintive cacophony
inside each *pot* gearing down for a light,
like an old tune striking up memories
of who he was, and what he is, and where,
back in the animal kingdom.

BUT THERE WERE MORNINGS

This evening, little left
for either of us to say,
you lie back in your recliner,
lift the tubing from the tank
and attach it to your nose,
as I wrestle with this weight,
duck-walking your refrigerator
out of the kitchen corner
to clean the floor behind it,
helping you prepare to move
nearer the Platte Valley, where you
once lived and have now decided
you will go home to die.

But there were mornings
we would rise before dawn,
hook up the boat and swing by
the truck-stop off the interstate,
buy large coffees, your cigarettes,
a tank-full of boat gas on our way
out to Elwood when it was new
and we were young enough to fish
all day from dawn to dusk,
drive back after dark and
clean our catch, then sleep
and wake to another of those mornings,
enough somehow this evening
to bear us through the night.

BLESSED SACRAMENT

On a rock outcropping in a fossil bed
four antelope drowse in the autumn sun,
until a bullet thumps like the fist of god
into the paunch of the male and he grunts;
a distant rifle pops and the startled does
burst all at once away to the south.

The buck, too shocked at first to rise,
comes up at the crunch of approaching boots,
leaps from the rock and lunges west
a quarter mile to the lip of a drop,
where his shoulders buckle and he rolls
but rises, clears a creek, emerges.

Slower now, his body humped, the deep
cramp tightening with every breath,
he stops at length on a ridge to rest,
turns and slowly eases down,
sees the man a half-mile back
drop out of sight in a wash in the dusk.

Twenty minutes later a silent flash
and the other fist of god thumps home,
the buck's erect neck slumps to the side
and what he was is gone, leaving
body and blood to feed his brother
kneeling with a knife at the earthen altar

in this, the first dark place of worship,
where every breathing thing still ends
a broken, bleeding Christ,
every keening mother, Mary,
burying her child of god.
It is *never* finished

THE WALKING WOUNDED

The winter after his good friend died
he pressed a loaded gun to his head,
fingered the narrow trigger and tried
to picture the rest, but not too hard,
just enough to imagine an end to pain,
a blotting out of those dark mishaps
that sooner or later stretch any chain
to the point where an over-stressed link snaps
and the story unravels, little matter
how hard one tries to hold it together,
the pieces of the old world fall away
into darkness, Peniel, Gethsemane,
where the few who wrestle through till dawn
arise, and wounded but awake, walk on.

THERE IS A FOUNTAIN
FILLED WITH BLOOD

That Lutheran hymn still comes to mind
when I recall her carrying him, big white rooster
my cousins raised from a fuzzy yellow chick
and named, like all their farmyard pets,
to the blood-stained chopping block that day
she hacked off his bewildered head,

nieces circling the gore, screaming,
"I *hate* you Auntie Stell! I *hate* you!"
headless body straining to voice
the obscene silence in her hand,
terminally naked neck become
a sudden fountain, spouting blood.

A rather common scene back then,
one way rural folks taught their young
how things work in this strange world,
where pets or people, loved or not,
every living thing must die
to feed some hunger on the earth.

I still remember watching, though
I forget that rooster's name.
Call him Immanuel.

SEASON OF THE LONG SHADOWS

In October
when the year begins
slowly sinking toward its end
face north
and close your eyes
on the path of the old migrations.

Hear lost echoes
of a feathered tide
rolling overhead in waves,
feel again
the ancient earth
cast into treeless shade for days.

See vast flocks
drawn to alluring calls
descend from the heavens and disappear,
as another living
piece of the planet falls
to the leveled guns of the marketeers.

POLYHYMNIA

She alone has the power to command
desolate madness, senseless fear,
the song of the wind in a wind-swept land

where high plains grasses swirl and bend
under timeless currents, a wild river
she alone has the power to command,

stripping the precious soils and sand
from the hills, from each unsheltered acre,
this dirge, the wind in a wind-swept land

rearranging earth like the very hand
of almighty God on this planet where
she alone has the power to command

the paths of the wandering clouds, and
so the floods, the droughts belong to her,
each a song on the wind in a wind-swept land,

a sacred echo, often deadly, and
as often sweet, no more than a whisper
from one who has the power to command
a song of the wind in a wind-swept land.

FOSTERING THE FUTURE

Under thrumming streets in the city of dreams
an unremembered stream harbors giant clams,
swollen foster mothers full of pale blue seeds
from windshields shattered into odd, sharp beads
that hail down daily from the storms above
and race toward their frigid folds of love,
hard, pearled wombs where they feed and grow,
developing a phosphorescent glow
that burns each host until at last
her dying lips open in a silent gasp,
exposing otherworldly globes of light
that cast first shadows on an ancient night,
their sick warmth rendering a toxic mix
of the once-pure waters of the river Styx.

SAILING WITH AHAB

Call me
what you will.

I was part of it,
drifting like you
above it all,

though no one asked me
what I thought
when it was going down,

and it was
going down
from the beginning,

but who could know
how far out we'd sail
on a sea of lies

in this hollow raft
now coming apart
in deep waters.

FAINT GLIMPSE OF THE GULF

"…there is a great gulf fixed: so that they which would
pass from hence to you cannot;"
—Luke 16:26

No science, no religion,
no theory or theology
handed down through the millennia
has bridged that timeless gulf between
thought and stark reality,
the eternal present, alive and well,
and ever out of reach in this
dream-world built of words.

Theorizing Bible scholars
found the ancient bones of science
merely manufactured lies,
while scientists kept the faith,
blind as Adam in the garden,
re-interring each fresh enigma
exhumed from the star-born earth
under the blank white stone of a name.

A shaken man lets his shovel fall
and whispers six simple syllables—
Tyrannosaurus Rex—and *it*
is gone, another trace of the mystery
paved smoothly over with words,
that life-long maze of detours
around the rough road in,
where there is no earth, no sea, no sky,
no world outside, no ear, no eye.

GREAT ROCKS IN GREEN LIGHT, LOST VOICES IN THEIR SHADOWS

Boulders three times taller than a man
shadow the meadow in thin green light
swallowing a brace of ducks in flight
over a pool above a beaver dam
where I fish perfect water in the rain,
anticipating camp, a pine-branch fire,
a bottle from which I'll try to pour
an answer commensurate with the pain
the damp earth whispers, a cup of warm,
complete release into memory,
where voices of an earlier century
descend on the meadow, emerging from
the groaning shadows, monolithic friends
on the floor of a dream that never ends.

THE LOST FISH

Nothing but the ripe sun's glare
off the surface of the still water, and then

standing high in the bow he sees
what has been so long invisible—fish

everywhere, and he throws the spear,
five useless tines disappearing

into the dark beneath the flash,
as the silver school slips away,

convincing him again that nothing
ever truly pierced such glass,

his brother silent at the oars, staring
over all they lost on this odd black lake,

where the myriad crooked streams spill out
like spokes in a wrecked bike wheel

from the fast-shrinking source of the rivers
that water the dying earth.

Something Precious
set it at the nho.
the Uncle takes the
Narrator there.

45

SOMEONE'S DESERTED IDEA
OF A HEAVEN

Somewhere in the past, or a dream
long past, a great white building
on a far-off hill, and my cousin and I,
bored with the familiar, one summer day
crossed Sunny Creek, a barbwire fence,
the neighbor's pasture, and climbed
the long way up that rise
to an ancient barn, no cows
in the pasture, no house or other buildings
there, no sign of life for years—
someone's deserted idea of a heaven
a long time lost, now desolate as hell.

We looked in all directions,
shivered as we circled the foreboding place,
egging each other on until
in we went, fully expecting
something terrible to rise from the dust
we stirred underfoot as we talked one another
into all but the blackest cob-webbed corners.

Climbing the ladder to the loft,
we eased over planks to a glassless window,
crawled out onto the rotten roof and stood
staring over the valley at the farms,
the distant houses, sheds, great barns, and
without a word we understood
all of it would mirror the ruin underfoot
one day when we were gone . . .

Off the roof, the loft, the ladder,
through the dark barn to the light at the door,
down the hill and through the fence,
we leapt the creek to familiar ground
and turned to face what we somehow knew
was trailing us, coming fast—
the barn, once small in the distance,
now like a seedling taking root,
draped the entire valley in its shadow.

So we began our race with death,
raising heart-felt, futile prayers
to a god we'd learned
had already died
a very long time ago.

OUT OF WHITE NOISE,
A SIREN SONG

Cynicism rises like a vampire
in the season of waning light.
A nine-o'clock visit to Walmart
and I'm ready to cross
even weekly shopping for groceries
off my reasons-to-leave-home list.

Fifty pounds of dog food on my back,
a dagger's worth of darkness in my heart,
I seek a quick exit from this white-noise world,
pinball past a bumper crop of shoppers,
get through self-checkout, then stagger out
to the bone-cold parking lot.

I catch a faint jingle by the main door
and see a big black man in a thin red suit,
Salvation Army bell in hand,
the lines of people streaming in and out,
flaring wide as wary geese
at a sour note from the call.

But the deep rhythm of his Christmas wishes
calls to my mind the musical cadence
of a drill sergeant just out of Viet Nam,
leading our platoon on a thirty-mile march
through the swelter of spring in Louisiana,

our all-green, multi-racial mass
echoing the music of a black man's voice,
prepared to follow that siren song
out of that swampland into the hills and
screaming jungles of a distant war.

I stow the dog food in the trunk,
glance once more at the man with the bell,
and fully aware things could be worse,
I buckle up, back out and face
the incoming lines of paired lights
on vehicles smoking like peasant torches
converging on some castle in the night.

THE LONG ACT OF FALLING

In a cotton shirt and cutoff jeans,
socks rolled over his boot-tops,
he crosses the New Fork on a fallen pine,
one of dozens spanning the river
at the crossing a mile and a half below
that steep descent on the Palmer Lake trail,
the long way down from Cutthroat Lakes.

Half-way across another of those trees
I stopped and snapped the photograph
I keep on the wall above my desk,
an eleven-by-fourteen black-and-white,
the best of those I shot back then,
an un-posed study of a friend, now dead,
crossing his last wild river.

Under the sun or the camera's magic
he appears outlined in fine bright light:
white hair, chin, the top of his pack,
shirt-front, forearm, hands, one thigh
ablaze in a silver, ghost-thin aura
as he leans forward, staring down
at the log ahead of his left foot,
fully considering his next step
atop that round and rotting bridge,

as if his life depends on it,
as though he sees the steps to come,
the diagnosis of the specialist,
surgery, a metal valve in a heart
long scarred from rheumatic fever,
then blood thinner, regular checkups and
the end of trekking into wilderness.

Beyond and above him, in its narrow cut,
the river runs black in a white-rock bed,
skirting boulders the size of old bulls
in its rush down that horizontal ladder of trees
toppled from the canyon walls where
three tall pines lean over the water
in the long act of falling.

WHAT HAVE I LEARNED

The car in the dark in the deep
shade in the 3rd level parking garage free
for those who have who know
someone inside the Center and so
obviously dying in one of the wards yet
never
mentioned in that artificial brightness
sterile rooms antiseptic halls
everyone straining smiling polite
as well-bred children thinking *if I'm good*
nothing bad will come
only
the occasional someone
screaming honest recognition
coming awake to the invisible flames
the jaws snapping shut on
the lure
the lie
forever falling
from a pulpit painting
the natural world a natural death
hell a dark and evil kingdom
coloring heaven a well-lit place
but
the paradox flowers
leaves one wanting and wanting
the exit out away

forever from brightness
please thank you
no more prayers *mercy* prolonging
this public pain this false
promise immortality
these sterile well-lit
realms forever
please
the *Exit* elevator down
out of the light at last in the deep
shade the garage the car
alone in the dark honestly
thankful whispering
Why am I here again?
What have I learned?

THINGS TO DO WHILE YOU'RE GONE

Water the flowers,
mow if needed,
feed your little dog,
laugh when you return,
travel to a distant school,
rent a cabin near a state park,
hurry to the office one afternoon,
take the call,
pack the car,
drive east until the motor dies,
flag a Sandhills rancher,
ask him to call for a tow,
wait an hour on the side of the road,
ride the tow-truck into town,
leave the car to cover the bill,
hitchhike back to the cabin,
wake the neighbor,
jump-start the pickup,
drive five-hundred miles,
and see you dying,
weep with the others,
pray to a remote god, but
imbibe the *local* spirits,
discover the uselessness of prayer,
take the long drive back to school,
curse religion,
leave the church,

drink for months, then
sober up,
go on,
live and
learn.

ON THE BLOCK WHERE I LIVE

I remember I followed my brother once
across the alley to a mountain of snow
piled beside the Mobil station on the corner,
and we made our assault on the steep north face,
up ragged chunks of dirt-caked ice
to the top, where we lingered, panting
but tall as the station's high block walls,
until a uniformed attendant spotted us,
stuck his head out the door and yelled,
and we leapt down in a graceless descent.

There's a beautiful park where that station stood,
spruce trees and roses where they piled the snow
those years before they tore the building down
and a drive-through bank went up on the corner
with a wide window where I'd always wave
at the cashiers on my way to the store,
and one or another of them would wave back,
until that morning, for no damned reason
they were all shot down while I slept.
I woke to sirens and the dismal news.

As a boy I dreamed heroic things,
and part of me wishes I'd awakened in time
to shoot it out with those hophead bastards,
too late of course to save a soul, it's little
more than vengeance. Still, some nights
I dream it—in the dark alley a hulking figure
shoots at me and I shoot back. He falls, and slowly
I stalk near, gun pointed at the back of his head
as I kick him hard in the side and wake
when I roll him over, and he's me.

BLACK-AND-WHITE

Three boys ankle-deep in prairie grass,
one with a dozen bullheads on a stringer,
a few fish seven or eight inches long,
some no bigger than a grown man's finger.

The license plate on the car behind them,
the baby moons, pronounced rear fenders
and little oval back window
place them in South Dakota in the forties.

Brothers, each bearing a share of that
ancient rivalry, they could almost pass
for white-haired men, caps shading their eyes, yet
unable to erase the darker shadows.

The youngest, on the right, six or seven
years old, wears overalls, a fur-collared coat,
and something of a smirk, the only one
portraying any pleasure in the scene.

Away to the left, the middle child,
in a worn-thin jacket and overalls,
aims a pained-soul frown at the camera
or the invisible cameraman.

Dead-center, the tallest boy, nine or ten,
in belted jeans and clean white shirt,
hoists the stringer in a high, tight fist, his
withering aspect pinched tight, scowling like a lord.

Cold as a silent curse, this photograph
mutes a sixty-year-old scream of all
they will become—old men, forever
unable or unwilling to forget.

OLD PHOTO OF "EDDIE"

In rolled-up shirt sleeves and rolled-up jeans,
big white western hat tipped back,
revealing your wealth of thick black curls,
you straddle some early boyfriend's bike
outside an old firehouse garage,
leaning forward on that vintage Harley,
grinning at the camera, mother's little sister,
looking fully ready for The Great Escape.

And if you'd known what lay ahead
you'd have kicked that cold machine to life
and roared away without one look back,
rolling out of reach of what no doubt was
already in hot pursuit and gaining fast,
decades of abandonment, poverty, pain,
leading to that illness doctors couldn't cure
and that death not one would speed.

LATE IN THE GAME

Gone now, like him, just a memory—
that sliver of moon against the Milky Way
lighting the pasture where my horses graze.

I stand on the porch at my brother's place,
tip back a bottle of foreign beer
and piss onto grass he hasn't mowed in years,
as I listen to the progress of the game.

Late in the fourth quarter, my brother's team
just tried a long field goal that failed to score,
and a loud curse rattles the closed screen door.

My dog slinks off the porch, through the gate,
and down beside the car she stretches out
on the hard gravel in my brother's lane
to await the eventual end of the game.

PRAYER FOR A PROPER DEATH

Let me be
active and alert
enough to see and hear it

coming down
sleek and wild
out of the Elysian hills

focused on
that singular hunger
knowing it must feed or die

and nothing now
will satisfy it
but the end of me.

III. THIS WILD PLACE

"It was then that I saw the flight coming on. It was moving like a little close-knit body of black specks that danced and darted and closed again. It was pouring from the north and heading toward me with the undeviated relentlessness of a compass needle."

—Loren Eiseley, "The Judgment of the Birds," *The Immense Journey*

THIS WILD PLACE

A spattered black iridescence
    feathers each small body
        floating
like a living heaven full of stars
    too far away to see
        in this
gathered storm of starlings filling
    the sky for the better
        part of an hour,
countless black flakes flurrying
    quietly over the creek and
        out
past the limited range of sight,
    an incomprehensible
        reality
virtually everywhere
    and wholly
        free,
out of reach of pale abstractions,
    our alphabets and
        digit strings,
words and numbers veiling wonders
    no human mind can name
        or know,
can only imagine
    tearing the curtain,
        and far

beyond these dull black marks,
    spattered multitudes of stars
      spanning
unbound time and space,
    raining endless
      waves of light,
the timeless burning
    pulse of it all
      in this wild place.

THEY CALLED THEM *BUFFALO*

Fingers curled in the thick chain-links
the boy leaned his head against the fence
and stared west through the woven wires,

letting go of time, of everything but being
one with those dark shapes and haunting moans,

great heads bowed to the summer grass
tall as his knees on the refuge hills
high above the river canyon,

and when at length he turned to ask,
and the others merely pointed and laughed
at the linked red dents in his forehead,

he turned back to the west,
to the face of God,

and loathe to be ignored,
they answered.

CLIMBING THE NIGHT

Once more on the forbidden stairs,
I'm climbing to the far stories
in the building with no ceiling,
down the hall of endless rooms,
to that familiar lamp-lit street
in the fog of a warm spring rain.

I remove my shoes and socks and take
the ten cold steps down damp concrete,
push hard against that massive door,
squeeze over the dim threshold and
shiver at the echoes as the great door
seals itself behind me.

Wet sand chills my feet
as I cross the midnight cave,
where something slithers quick and cold
beneath my heel and I coil and leap
toward a faint light in a narrow tunnel
where outsize paw marks pock the sand.

Following the cave to its dim-lit mouth,
on hands and knees in the fading dusk,
I hear them calling one to another,
great cats in broken country
moving back to their lair.

Then my lost dog is bounding toward me,
leaping, whining, leading me out
to another light inside a ring of rocks
where the roaring stops and a strange familiar
wrapped in shadow and a hooded robe
beckons once and moves away.

And I know I will never see that face
or understand that alien tongue,
but I will follow, mark every move,
and learn again the forgotten way
back to the farther circles.

WOLF-SONG HEART

in memory of Louis Owens

Behind my aging dog this evening,
I watch her thinning, wire-haired body
scuttle down the bike trail south of town,
heading west in her angular trot
past fields of freshly-disked corn stubble,
a stout wind dusting the tin-gray sky,
trees along the trail just starting to bud.

She slips into last year's knee-high grass
along the shoulder and fades from sight
like her namesake, Smoke, then reappears
tracking something in the fence-line brush
to a sudden point where she drops and rolls—
Let it be, I yell in her direction, but
she emerges chewing on a scrap of deer-hide.

And I can't help smiling, unable to conceal
my respect for her immediate response to hunger,
echo of that still-wild song in her heart
ringing out here in the open air, where
the eternal pulse of life-and-death
reflects an enigma far beyond
the sorely stunted range of human diction.

And though I realize these odd black marks
must fall as short as a novice newsman's
attempt to convey a sense of *hurricane*
from a desk in sunny Iowa, here
where the praises of prairie wolves still
echo down the wild heart of Mystery,
I've found my personal Savior.

IN THE COMPANY OF EAGLES

Mid-march along Lost Lamb Creek,
a spring-fed series of hayfield ponds
stacked like stairs behind stick dams,

two hulking shadows unfurl and sail
off the high boughs of a cottonwood, and
hordes of mallards slap from the surface
of the frigid waters and climb.

BECAUSE

each autumn she runs the yucca-clustered hills,
this ancient grassland full of prickly pear and prairie rose,
ranging ahead, casting left and right,
reveling in the scents, as meadowlarks
and mourning doves lift up and out of reach,
deer and coyotes slip away unseen, and
jackrabbits challenge her to open-country races
we all three know she can't win,
but know too she has to follow, because

out here, away from the common
chaos of the streets in the city where we live,
she can hear again a voice within
calling her back to her birthright,
the uncluttered wild, where everything is
a simple coupling, predator and prey,
every scent a call to grace—*Follow me*—
and nose down, tail aquiver,
without question she obeys, because

this way is narrow and she knows
it leads to the holy of holies,
the eternal present, where she locks on point,
silent, motionless, eye-to-eye,
pointer and sharptail a single being
lost in timeless meditation
before the inevitable sacrifice—a grouse
bursts skyward, my dog leaps after, and I
wake from this trance and raise the gun, because

EVENING ON THE ELKHORN

for Bill and Julia

The sun dips to the magic angle
and the downstream riverbanks start to glow
that sudden once-in-the-long-day green,
as over the receding flood we ride,

our canoe skirting massive root wads,
whole trees hung on emerging sandbars
where great blue herons stand spearing minnows
from brown swirls of April water.

A snowy egret climbs quiet as a cloud,
loud pairs of Canadas honk and rise,
and from the high heavens a dark hawk
unlocks its talons, teaching a snake to fall.

As we pull ashore for a late picnic
a giant bird glides over the water
and lands in a snag on the other side,
the low sun setting its breast ablaze.

When we launch again, it lofts, a golden eagle
dodging the swift black sorties of a crow
and fading with the sun, a final set of wings
waving as we leave the river.

BETTER FISHING

Late November, a narrow crust of ice
along either bank of the Missouri River, and
we'd caught nothing but a couple of drum
below the dam up on Gavin's Point.

So I folded the trolling motor onto the bow,
my neighbor yanked the Merc to life,
and we nosed the boat downstream to take
one final stab at better fishing.

I was pouring coffee, and he'd unwrapped a sandwich,
when we came around a bend and found the congregation,
two dozen bald eagles on a wide sandbar, a few standing stoic,
others hopping about, fighting over a pair of dead fish.

He dropped the sandwich and reached for his camera,
easing the boat toward the South Dakota side,
but with a violent thumping of wings they paired up
and peeled away on updrafts, far above the river.

When we looked back down at each other, we shook our heads.
Coffee cold, sandwich soggy, no fish, no photos,
we swung the boat around and gunned back toward the dock,
laughing and joking and recounting the long day.

And somehow I can't remember better fishing.

MAGDALENE LAKE

He packed into wilderness
mid-summer in the Bighorns,
up to Brown Bear Lake
and down to Magdalene,
unrolled a sleeping bag
on the floor of a one-man tent,
left the rain-fly off
so he could study the stars.

A night with no mosquitoes
he tied the tent door open
and stared at constellations
he had never seen before, or
never seen so clearly
those miles down on the plains,
as the vast earth moved beneath him
slow as the hour hand of a clock.

He dozed at last in the night,
a speck as insignificant
as a specimen under glass,
though what looked down
he could not know,
could only sense it,
cold and wild,
when he awoke
and wondered.

PLATTE VALLEY GIRLS

for Ashley and Shelby and Kasey and Paige

When the robins wake you in the spring,
lie in bed a moment, listening
to their sweet voices beneath your own
breathing in that peaceful space, your home.

When the summer frogs on the river start
chanting lullabies, each taking part
in that ancient chorus at the long day's end,
close your eyes and drift home with them.

And late in autumn when the geese begin
their long ride south on the cold north wind,
each of them urging the others on
as they follow the arc of the planet down,

let your spirits rise and fly with them,
back with your sisters to your home, within.

POET

The Muse comes finally down
the slow road to perception,
singing, dancing,
leading you
to the lip of a black crevasse,
where bottomless warnings echo
the voices of ancient fathers,
gods you were taught to obey.

Bow, now,
and turn away,
or plunge headlong into the dark
and follow the familiar drumming back
down to that prodigal welcome where
the Mother of your pulse awaits.

LEARNING ALL THE TIME

Sometimes I bring odd things to class,
impossible propositions like—*study*
every tree in the world and you won't find any
two exactly the same—and there's really
no way I can prove that's true, but odds are
no one else can prove it's not, considering
the space/time continuum and the symbiotic
link between genetics and environment.

So, smug as any fool known to unleash
his personal theories on the unsuspecting,
I'm drawn one day to take a more in-depth
look at my front-yard maple, the one I tend
to ignore those countless times each year
I step out for the mail or the evening news,
drive under in my car, coming or going,
shovel snow off the sidewalk beneath,
or circle again and again each summer
with the mower, thankful for the shade.

And for the first time I really see this thing—
fat roots clinging to the four directions
at the base of a trunk eight-foot around
that rises five feet and forks into three
thick boughs that fork another foot higher
into dozens of arm- and leg-thick limbs,
each climbing a short way to fork again
into wrist-thick branches, then fingerling
twigs that fork at last into myriad stems,
each ending in a unique leaf, and suddenly
a more specific theorem occurs to me—
that's one strange forking tree.

MID-OCTOBER EVENING

for Kathleen

After a long day hunting Sandhills grouse
we're driving back along the Beaver Creek,
beat, but content with the familiar aches
under sweat-soaked clothes beginning to cool,

when a vast curtain of birds is drawn
at dusk across the sky over the gravel road,
a seeming endless cloud of massed starlings,
pouring out of the north and spilling away

into the south as far as we can see,
their combined chorus deafening
as the noise of some un-invented machine
running a final harvest on the earth,

reminiscent of that old Hitchcock film,
the avian element of the globe gone wild,
a possible outcome of our present fix
in a world growing ever more polluted and warm,

ripe perhaps for the plagues a young Moses
called forth from the heart of a jealous god,
bent on freeing a long-enslaved people
from oppression in a too-proud land, where

we're told a hard heart doomed a pharaoh's army,
as surely as those flocks that once eclipsed the sun
were soon felled by limitless market hunting,
streaming down a river of no return,

yet even as such thoughts cross my mind,
the birds keep winging on, into the night,
and at heart I know they are no more, no less
than the rarest of blessings at the end of day.

BADLANDS

Another callous christening,
another careless judgment passed
on a vital part of the living world.
Who gave this place that name?

Fear once more the initial response
to the face of the vast unknown,
names uttered in the vain attempt
to divide this inscrutable world
into good and badland places.

Black Hills winds, rains and snows
fused in the fourth dimension
rise dense as a nuclear cloud,
towering miles of drops and flakes
unearthing the ragged pages of time.

Unfathomed rivers of erosive power
jig-saw an otherwise dead planet
into fitting niches for myriad forms
of that enigma, life, still emerging
from the waters of a basement sea.

Bluegill, rattlesnake, sharptail, pronghorn,
the glorious chain of mysteries goes on
swimming, crawling, flying, running
flat-out across this ocean prairie,
itself a product of the august sun.

A lone coyote hunting the twilight
pauses to celebrate his momentary link
with the whole of the sacred world in this
best left unnamed place.

"DERBY HORSE"

after Deborah Butterfield's sculpture

Elemental color, monumental sheen,
metallic link in a species' progression
along a chain of three- and four-toed shadows
forged in the fires of the <u>Eocene</u>   *Eohippus*
from the unalloyed bones of the early ones—
Hyracotherium, Orohippus,
Mesohippus, Merychippus, Calippus,
Pliohippus, Pseudohipparion,
Hipparion, Neohipparion—
your names ring down the millennia
as the rumble of your odd and countless hooves,
the beating of your wild and ancient hearts
echo in this metal cage of ribs
and your race against the night goes on . . .

No creature plans its Evolution.
There's no mind calculating
survival, only the odds
some better, some worse
carry a beast farther
than any others

OLD HABITS

Into the blossoming essence of April,
my twelve-year-old dog leads me out to the trestle,
and we head west between white-flowered thickets,
the wild plums abloom either side of the trail.

Unleashed at last from the day's cares, I run
out of old habit, like a dog in a dream
tracking down a long-gone litter of pups and
fetching them back one or two at a time—

Happy and Lucky, Tiny and Snowball,
Willie and Nikki, Kelly and Ace,
Pee-Wee, both Peppers (one spotted, one black),
Fred and Barney, Duke, the two Belles,

Cory, Yoda, Rowdy, Rusty,
Rocky, Aries, Aspen and Trey,
Mattie, Emmet, Jenny, Blizzard,
Buddy, the Gypsy—each of them rare,

a perfect misfit in a misshapen pack
of pedigreed pointers, coonhounds, retrievers,
a cross-bred assortment of happenchance mutts,
howlers and barkers, bay-ers, yarkers,

beggars and stealers, old lollygaggers,
bold tail-sniffers, wild trouble-makers,
loafers and tireless pissers of tires,
each without question a best-friend for life.

Out to the feedlot and back to the trestle,
trailing Smoke, the living heart of the pack,
I hear in the blossoming rasp of her panting
the approach of the dreamer that will fetch us all home.

CADENCE

I tell the class poetry is spoken art
based on the musical rhythms of words,
and long before we ever learn to write
our original sense of the world relies
less on intended meaning than on sound.

Sounds are what we remember, I suggest, and
nodding toward a sophomore who's in the Reserves
I sing out—*You had a good home but you left . . . .*

Stark silence ensues, a row of odd stares,
but in my mind I pick it up—*You're right!*
and once more I'm in a column of troops
echoing a drill sergeant's cadence—

Hi-ho diddly-bop,
    Hi-ho diddly-bop,
I wish I was back on the block,
    I wish I was back on the block,
with my cane pole in my hand,
    with my cane pole in my hand,
I'm gonna be one fisher-man,
    I'm gonna be one fisher-man,
Yo lef-right,
    Lef-right,
Oh lef-right,
    Lef-right,
Hi-ho diddly-bop . . .

A long moment passes in silence
as those old echoes rise in me
and I consider sounding off again,

but there's no way to share with them
full surrender to a drill sergeant's cadence
on a thirty-mile march in a three-year hitch—

they'll be back on the block in an hour.

THE HORSES OF HAZELWOOD

for Desmond Egan

The Outdoor Light with the photos of those grand
horses and the artist who carved them, your friend
James McKenna, brought a sense of your loss,

that hollow feeling dreams so often cause
when they fade like the sweet scent of lumber,
the careful chocking of chisel and hammer

gone silent at the end of building
what cannot last and is already bleeding
its fine light back into the fertile earth,

though the artist clearly found it worth
the deliberate pains he brought to bear
on works erected in the open air,

where he knew time would take it all apart
and reunite the artist with his art.

THE FIRST TIME

Stranger, I followed you down to the light,
drawn by the printed echo of your words,
your lonely work the resurrection of worlds
gone cold as ghost stars haunting the night,
old fires resolute as a dead man's mind
still casting shadows of his sojourn here,
so infinitesimal, and yet so near,
caught forever in the firmament of time.
Into the night, that ancient country,
I followed the eerie echoes down,
spent strange hours amid the runes and found
only an alias, *Eiseley*,
in the ruins of that deep enigma,
your apocrypha, America.

. . . AND GOLDEN NEEDLES

A few days after they burned the state grass
off the field between this crescent of lakes,
I imagine the clumps of shoulder-high stalks
as they began to crackle, became a low roar,

wild flames rising, stalking the field
like a hungry beast, trailing smoke,
leaving nothing but a few burnt saplings
scattered across a thick carpet of ash.

I follow my dog this April evening
across the field's soft black mat,
drawn to the calls of Canada geese
paired up on the banks of the spring-fed lakes,

the fire-born seeds already sprouted,
and everywhere through the short green clumps
a suspended maze of webbing so fine
it would be invisible in any other light.

Just now, near dusk, the angle of the sun
illuminates this laser-thin feat of engineering,
and something here feels strangely mended by
these interminable miles of silver threads.

INVISIBLE GODS

Her urgent whispers lead him over
fading tracks of a recent coyote
to the warm sand of a hidden blowout

across a fence long gone to rust
on the earth divided eons ago
into *Private Property! Mine! Keep Out!*—

each sign a flaming sword at the gate
to that singular paradise, *here-and-now*,
outlawed forever though still within reach,

in the ripe shade of a forbidden tree,
where they once more embrace and fall,
in obvious spite of the writers of rules,

and consummate the ultimate trespass,
bold as the invisible gods.

THIS ANIMAL

She pounces and chews on a tennis ball
when I kneel on the rug in the living-room
to stretch my legs before our morning run
along the river on the new bike trail
they poured over the defunct U. P. line,
where she'll head west along the right-of-way
and I'll follow, conscious of her leading me
out of complacence and once again
into a world she can sense somehow, still
blooming at the end of that ancient track,
and I know if I let her take me back,
let the rotten fruits of knowledge fall
like crusted scales from a blind man's eyes,
I'll be with her today in paradise.

BLUEBIRD AFTERNOON

A fall day, the sky a clear and bottomless blue,
what the outdoor-magazine experts called
bluebird weather, no day for ducks,

but I was young, with little time for experts,
just a need to be out on the river with a gun,
and first-hand knowledge of local wood ducks
whistling over backwaters on bluebird afternoons.

I walked in from the county road,
thumbing three 20-gauge number 4's,
pale yellow shells with bright brass heads,
into Mom's old Marlin pump.

The trail through the trees lay ankle-deep
under a coat of many colored leaves,
but a wild thumping in my chest
drowned out the sound of my approach.

Then over the high cottonwoods they came
whistling, and I drew a quick lead and fired,
saw my first duck crumple all at once and fall
with a soft crash onto the brittle leaves.

I ran to find a wood duck drake,
a burst of colors unbelievable but real,
and knelt there, trembling on the silent
floor of the otherwise vacant world.

Now, it's like some stage I stood on
once, on a bluebird afternoon, or
some episode in a mental film
I can play back now and contemplate,

or maybe it's just me,
and maybe it always was,
here, now, doing this.

SOMEWHERE THIS MORNING

Salmon climb
a still-wild river,
red waves
ripe to spawn and die
up near the source of waters,
sky,
    above the hulking
grizzly shadows
slashing at each shallow frenzy
ascending the unforgotten fork,
this
    selfless mass of finned Christs
struggling back to spend themselves
in that crystal stream where they began
the long ride down to the sea.

CPSIA information can be obtained at www.ICGtesting.com
Printed in the USA
BVOW020056300312

286384BV00001B/40/P